CONCENTRATE

CONCENTRATE

Poems

Courtney Faye Taylor

WINNER OF THE CAVE CANEM POETRY PRIZE
SELECTED BY RACHEL ELIZA GRIFFITHS

Graywolf Press

Copyright © 2022 by Courtney Faye Taylor
Introduction copyright © 2022 by Rachel Eliza Griffiths

"Black Korea." Words and Music by O'Shea Jackson. Copyright © 1991 Universal Music Corp. and Gangsta Boogie Music. All Rights Administered by Universal Music Corp. All Rights Reserved Used by Permission. *Reprinted by Permission of Hal Leonard LLC.*

This publication is made possible, in part, by the voters of Minnesota through a Minnesota State Arts Board Operating Support grant, thanks to a legislative appropriation from the arts and cultural heritage fund. Significant support has also been provided by the McKnight Foundation, the Lannan Foundation, the Amazon Literary Partnership, and other generous contributions from foundations, corporations, and individuals. To these organizations and individuals we offer our heartfelt thanks.

Published by Graywolf Press
212 Third Avenue North, Suite 485
Minneapolis, Minnesota 55401

All rights reserved.

www.graywolfpress.org

Published in the United States of America

ISBN 978-1-64445-210-3 (paperback)
ISBN 978-1-64445-193-9 (ebook)

2 4 6 8 9 7 5 3 1
First Graywolf Printing, 2022

Library of Congress Control Number: 2022930733

Cover design: Courtney Faye Taylor

Cover art: Mark Clennon, *Mother and Child*; Asia Rivera

Contents

Introduction

A poet cups her hands around a flame that breathes its own genesis. Her voice carries from this fire, from the paths that line the palms of her hands, from the breath that will carry her forward on a pilgrimage that will lead her to paradise.

Here is her voice: "So far my sentence as a Black woman has been   hard to hone, homed in sore white pith. Put graciously, Black womanhood has been a limb that's fallen asleep beneath me, paddy wagon of spinal cords in Baltimore's traffic up ahead. This whole color was a mistake—a leak in the ceiling whorehouse, a confused ass whooping."

Inside the flesh of her hands, Courtney Faye Taylor carves her own image against her birth, which belongs firstly to herself, and with exhalation blazes in every direction of her powerful debut, *Concentrate*. The light of the poet's wisdom and rage is a match, lit and sustained, in a body of work that scrapes like flint against the palms and skulls of her ancestors. In the earth of her voice, Taylor incinerates the trifling tools of the masters who have attempted to dismantle her existence.

Arriving fully formed, wholly vulnerable, here at the threshing floor of her own body, it is evident to me and to her audience that Taylor's presence hails from what is most sacred to the life and calling of a poet. This calling is intimate, universal, and dangerous.

In *Concentrate*, Taylor withstands the negative space that surrounds her memory, both private and collective, aware that her breath and the history of what is tradition (and what isn't) are all conjured of the most delicate, flammable, and combustible brilliance. This first book of poems, which centers the lives, deaths, and unsayable memories of Black girls and Black women, claps back against erasure, amnesia.

This confrontation is a language, a luster that is as much about home as the petroleum jelly a Black girl uses to coat her face, knees, elbows, and soft limbs before facing the world beyond the doors of her home, which is as much about her body as her shelter and refuge. Taylor celebrates and probes how Black girls receive their birthrights and education, which are often passed down through rituals of care, defense, protection, beauty, and performance.

I picture the poet removing her earrings before this battle. I picture her soaking her mind in a spiritual bath, the oceans inside of her filled with poultices, wings, bones, and the screams of her mothers, fathers, sisters, daughters, and unborn kin rising from the blood that floats in our history and memory.

I see Taylor polishing her platinum crown that her ancestor James Baldwin has reminded us has already been bought and paid for. Her language shines red and gold with blood, iron, salt, and the alloy of grace, steeped in craft and courage.

Concentrate explodes with meaning, explicit and implied. Courtney Faye Taylor understood Audre Lorde's assignment—"when we speak we are afraid / our words will not be heard / nor welcomed / but when we are silent / we are still afraid // So it is better to speak."

This is a first book of poems about a living Black girl who aims her lovesong—which is, too, a ghost story—at what could have easily been her own fate. Taylor centers the brief life and killing of another Black girl named Latasha Harlins, who was shot at age fifteen by Soon Ja Du, a Korean grocery store shopkeeper, in South Central, Los Angeles, California.

While this is the central spinal cord of Taylor's collection, the nerve endings of *Concentrate* extend in all directions: past, present, and future. In 1991, Harlins's death would become part of the psychic fling that provoked the Los Angeles Riots after the acquittal of four Los Angeles Police Department officers who were videotaped during the brutal beating of Rodney King. Harlins's murder happened thirteen days after King's beating.

This is the history, the shallow grave of what could be called Fact. Yet Taylor breathes flesh into what is unknown or barely visible. Organized in seven sections, she will stretch, splice, and speculate as to how prejudice, fear, and desire afflict memory and history. How does memory gird body? How does memory incubate fear amid communities of color and how do such communities endanger themselves, risking far more than what they will nearly work themselves to death to receive: an identity that is lodged in the precincts of the white imagination?

The poet wades into an uneasy ocean of interrogations that do not permit her any distance from what she has witnessed her entire life. Tireless and often devastating, the poet works to understand the language that seeks to shut down her dreams, bury her and her worth in illegible, transactional documentation. In these poems you can literally feel Taylor's mind racing, collapsing, deconstructing, and reconstructing paradigms that will allow her oxygen, freedom, imagination. The poet demands something beyond mere survival.

Taylor raises her voice so that we must listen. *Who was* Latasha Harlins and *who loved* her?

Innovative, inventive—qualities that are cellular blueprints for Black women—Taylor pours flame upon flame, willing sometimes to immolate herself in wonder and reckoning, particularly in her awareness of what she has been taught and what she must learn. For Taylor, *Concentrate* is a vision, arriving as a constellation, a Greek chorus or Baptist choir, a birthright, a labor forced upon Black women's lives before they've barely begun to recognize their own beautiful faces in the warped surface of storefront windows.

Taylor is our sister, our tutor, our jury, our sketchbook artist. I see her—a young Black girl who sweeps up clouds of Black hair left on the floors of courtrooms, beauty salons, bodegas, classrooms, interstates, morgues, sidewalks, and even more painfully, sometimes within our own homes. The poet scrubs at the blood, aware that this blood is her blood. The message burns her even as she holds herself inside of cold, freezing flames, risking her own safety to say it loud.

For this body of work is not the easy work of love but its necessary ancestor. I sense, for Taylor, that there can be no other way for such a call to arms. And this insight, and its troubling, is the long-anticipated breath that belongs to the ceaseless litany of Black imagination, in all of its Diasporic incantations.

Concentrate resists the monolithic, the static. Instead, Taylor is symphonic, kinetic, kismet. She begins her task with a poem, "So far," which is about the interior landscape of Black womanhood and the visceral journey of what it might mean to lay hands on her own life, aware that her own voice and the threat of violence is omnipresent, the charmed hook of the song.

The poet questions every sanctuary, whether that is a young Black girl sitting between the knees of a beloved auntie who is trying to tell her how to save herself from the world, or the arms of a man who will violate her trust, as well as her body, over and over again in her own home.

The section *"Arizona?"* is a scene, dramatic and complicated, whose dialectical refrains and chorus are reminiscent of the heartbreaking scene between Janie Crawford and her granny in Zora Neale Hurston's *Their Eyes Were Watching God*. In Taylor's poem, Aunt Notrie is a wary Virgil, who feels it is her responsibility to "educate" her niece about the suffering and violence she can expect to encounter beyond the safety and tenderness in her home. The irony and familiar archetype of this dialogue involves the niece holding her ears and inhaling the scent of her own burnt hair as she is ordered by Aunt Notrie to both listen and hold her head down so that her natural hair can be straightened out.

Like the word *Concentrate*, the word *Arizona* becomes loaded and unfamiliar. The use of it is weaponized, like the hot comb in Aunt Notrie's hands, and possesses the ability to scorch her niece. The act of listening is charged, heated. The speaker is talking about the kind of tea Trayvon Martin was carrying when he was killed. Latasha Harlins was killed because the Korean grocery store shopkeeper believed that the girl was trying to steal some orange juice despite the fact that Latasha had the money to pay for it.

In this book the sensation of brokenness is, and isn't, tender. There are complicated, irresolvable questions at stake. Taylor pivots from glazing over suffering with glory or the Strong Black Woman syndrome. The glory you'll find here is the desire of one Black girl to love, to save, and to remember another Black girl. Lift her name out of an unmarked mass grave of Black bones buried in a cemetery called Paradise.

This is ambitious work, uninterested in showing off (because it does dazzle, innately and organically). Rather, this is an *immersive* work, elevating the infrastructure of the mind in such a way that leaves you changed. You'll find yourself looking with suspicion at what is familiar and seeing, through Taylor's voice, what and who is really looking back at you. The sanctity of the gaze is ever tenuous. Taylor brings us to the brink, in the form of images and language. She binds mythos and meaning against each other until something breaks. We cannot, these poems demand, be comfortable. We must be reminded that we are each capable of a dire complicity at the hands and language of others, and by our own tongues and hands. Surveillance is not a binary but a matrix, a mythos, filled with conceits and optical illusions. This incandescent body of work asks, "For whom?"

I adore Taylor's boldness, her reclamation of a cosmos that is both revelatory, unbothered, and unbossed. I hear Toni Morrison's anthem, "You your own best thing, Sethe. You are."

I hear Toni Cade Bambara's shattering inquiry, "Are you sure, sweetheart, that you want to be well? Just so's you're sure, sweetheart, and ready to be healed, cause wholeness is no trifling matter. A lot of weight when you're well." I think of the postcard that Nikky Finney received from Bambara, instructing the poet "do not leave the arena to the fools."

Reading *Concentrate*, I sense Taylor has carved an entire arena of her own. Fools and foolishness be damned.

Salvation, these poems assure us, is not a state of grace, per se, but an action, a will. Change can happen by close reading and closer living to what we say we are willing to do, be. *Concentrate* is deliberate in its imagination and action.

Courtney Faye Taylor pushes us beyond the poetics of language into a symphonic atmosphere that requires listeners and readers, more willful and wild in our minds. She has breathed into the past and offered her blood and tongue as testament, as a prophecy of the future.

And, for me, it is utterly breathtaking whenever I repeat Taylor's question to the bright, salt-stained air that will outlive us both: "What girl of color survives // what happens?"

The poet has joined her courage to something far more dangerous, which is love.

Rachel Eliza Griffiths

CONCENTRATE

They are left to imagine
what her life might have been.
We are left to imagine the day
it won't require imagination

—KAMILAH AISHA MOON

So far my sentence as a Black woman has been   hard to hone, homed in sore white pith. Put graciously, Black womanhood has been a limb that's fallen asleep beneath me, paddy wagon of spinal cords in Baltimore's traffic up ahead. This whole color was a mistake—a leak in the ceiling whorehouse, a confused ass whooping. You see the baby in the blinds, the eager run in nylons, a public school lisp making room for the velour of her name. I was one of them. In grade school. It seemed my whole class had fallen asleep in front of a microwave. I drew faces on my galas then ate them off. God to me was my distantly gentle Aunt Notrie; brilliant completely, Virginia Slims and breadsticks, the shade on her side of Brewster slouched the coolish way a suburb deserves. Sunday, she was an usher with one breast. I crept to mom 'n' pops where bells above doors snitched to mention my entrance. But I tolled them bells. I was toys to be bothered. I had made such toyish mistakes. In any Black sentence, you'd love nothing more than to had made   no mistake.

Arizona?

The Talk

[Aunt Notrie in a chair, me between her knees. My hair's getting pressed. We speak.]

< *keep still now*

> I'm trying to.

< Ain't about *trying*, it's about *doing*. How
else you plan to survive? Live a life of
trying and you just end up tried . . .
All that child was tryna buy
was a drink.

> Arizona?

< South Central. You wasn't even
thought of yet, so just
let me tell it—*tilt your head
toward me*

> I mean Arizona tea. What that
boy held in a hoodie with Skittles,
not a knife?

< Boys ain't the only cause of chalk-
lines. You got that allergy to sixteenth
birthdays too, understand?—*sit up
straight*—This was OJ.

> Deaconess Pat poured us cups out
that "from concentrate" jug and, on
God, the pulp in that stuff taste—

< Did that deaconess teach you the longest
meaning of concentrate?—*hold your ear
down*—A strong, hard focus. Not at all
like when I'm talking safety and you
stuck on sweets.

> yes, ma'am.

< Girl named . . . Latrice? Had two dollars
for juice but the grocer had an itch to
shoot somebody.

> White men live to shoot somebody.

< No th—*girl, i done told you be
   still now*—the shot came out a woman.
   She of a color but   not ours.

                                                    > Other colors killing us like
                                                       white men now?

< A Korean woman kills like
   a Korean woman—*turn left*
   You not hearing me. I'm tryna
   save you, but I oughta just—*left,
   girl!*—I oughta

            just slap you.

~~Did Mrs. Du react inappropriately? Absolutely. But was that overreaction understandable? I think it was.~~ To suggest that any sentence that this court might give results in the conclusion that young black children don't receive full protection of the law—I'm sorry, but that is dangerous...unjustified. It is now a time for healing. It is not a time for rhetoric, which serves no purpose other than to fuel the fire. It's like throwing gasoline on ~~a fire that's already burning. It is~~ my opinion...Does society need Mrs. Du to be incarcerated in order to be protected? I think not. I know a criminal when I see one. I know a person who presents a danger to the community when I see one.

When I don't, I treat that person as something other..."

"tell me what's a black life worth a bottle of ~~[lemon]~~ is no excuse the truth hurts."

OVER JUICE

"One child grows up to be somebody that just loves to learn..."

Koreans join hands to heal wounds

Blacks and

"[Latino family looting]: not an uncommon sight..."

"Korean grocer gets probation FOR KILLING BLACK TEEN."

"...show the U.S. majority society the hard-working character of Koreans."

"Koreans have been the scapegoats of Black-White problems."

"you see, it's in the blood."

"$500 fine, 5 years probation FOR KILLING A 15 YEAR OLD."

AMERICAN GIRL

"Can we all get along?"

"hordes of young people"

"...an able and respected race."

"American Dream has been shattered [for Koreans]."

"I'm lucky they didn't kill me!"

~~"I'm lucky they didn't kill me!"~~

"Blacks, Whites join."

"Looting was a family affair." | a family affair a family a | hongry wolvs of pray ho

excessive force excessiv

POLICE RESPOND FAIL

"Blacks looting with RECKLESS abandon."

"hungry wolves of prey."

"...the wolves of ordinary [White] citizens."

54 deaths | 300 hurtings | 3,600 fires

"Tupac said her name."

"It was a family affair."

police failed to respond to calls

"black, but oj"

"You can't cry 'cause you'll look broke down... But you're cryin' anyway 'cause you're all broke down."

"And another child grows up to be somebody you'd just love to burn."

"Can we all get along?"

$1.79

"...an able and respected race."

"Looting was a family affair."

"Slayed teen was connected to the OJ trial in a couple of ways. ...OJ in a couple of ways."

< I was living in a #WarZone for quite some time. Caught up and
called to instigate, God would be sitting on my shoulder then just
stop. I'm telling you, after I bruised in Bally Fitness, fools pulled seven
melees across the tristate. There was people in a famine—maybe
you—and you ain't know race was a widow. You ain't care. Race was
your window. Smelly braids behaved fancy. Doses locked by 10:00 p.m.
You'd stare at the ceiling, breaking rye, cheering the Bruins—*move your
hand*—it's true. Ask and I'll drive ya ass to homeland where
they hold up the Samsung and riot for *no indictment*. Smoke boycotts
our family behind seven megaphones across that state. By now
there are percussionists in the bloodline, driven to homicide, caught
up in some stuff. Maybe it's you.

< In the riots, the unthinkable got thought of   then done.

In that zip code, "mad" could mean "very much."

On the radio, the wronged got rude and tuneful.
I remember the raps—*head back*—Ice Cube's "Black

Korea."

every time I wanna go get a fuckin' brew I gotta go down to the store with the two Oriental one penny countin' motherfuckers

Kierra cause a little ruckus

Tanequa try to rob

NO Refund Exchange ONLY

STORE POLIC...

NO CASH REFUND (EXCHANGE OR STORE CREDIT) *RECEIPT REQUIRED

* NO EXCHANGE FOR THE THINGS TO BE SANITIZED (WIGS, DRAW STRINGS, ETC.)

* EXTRA ATTENTION ON CHILDREN IN ORDER TO PREVENT DAMAGE ON PRODUCTS (DAMAGE COMPENSATION)

DO NOT PUT FULL WIGS ON WITHOUT ... CAP (5 0.50 /PC)

Thinkin' every brother
in the world's out to
take so they watch every
damn move that I
make.

...ut bitch, I got a J O B

So don't follow me up and down your market your little chop suey ass'll be a target

They hope I don't pull out a **GAT**

Tanequa → Shop lifter

funky little store

Kierra → Driver accomplice

that make a nigga mad eno...

Juice with the people, that's what the boy got

> Y'all was mad forever?

< "Forever" a fraught word, ain't it? Had no
  wound potential till milk stopped running
  ads for the snatched—*look here, you can
  either play with that phone or get your damn
  hair done. which is it gon' be?*

> sorry.

< Back then, missing flyers were a
  mama's cardstock anxieties pinned
  to phone poles, petting the air. I'd rip

  them down on my walks to work then
  cut and paste the faces wild . . . One girl's
  nose on some other lady's mug, snaggletooth
  on a vet, plait on

  a prostitute. They'd be last seen wearing
  all kinds of blue, costume jewels, some
  distant country's hair. Why a flyer mentions
  a sista's belongings is beyond me. We know

  she'll turn up dead or devastated   with none of it on.

Chesimard may wear h

earing a blue short-s, flowered shirt

dark blue or black shirt, black

blue sweat

blue jeans.

cavities.
previously

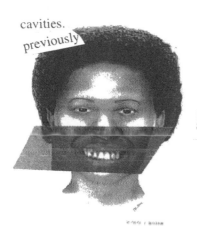

Sex: Female
Race: Black
Hair Color: Black
Eye Color: Black

This is a life-like computer generated image rendering, created by LSU. LA. Reference number is LSU 12-03. Age and height are approximates. Do not eliminate a victim strictly based on these attributes.

, jewelry was found. The victim had some dental work completed on her teeth.

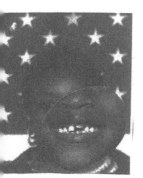

CONSIDERED

N ESCAPE

Occupation/Lifestyle: Landscaper,
Construction/Laborer,
Housekeeper, Prostitute, Drug User

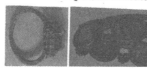

< Shoot, girl! Fooling around with you I done
   lost my place.

> You was saying *Koreans, turn left, I
   oughta slap you.*

< Right around nine. That's when—Letitia?
   Latoya? something like that—shook the store
   bell for a little swig of juice. $1.79. Had two
   to pay. Got popped in the head anyway.

> I wish hot combs could rake the race
   off our endings.

< She was wearing dickies, a Brui—
   sit back—a Bruins cap, lime green
   backpack. Not a hoodie, hear me?
   Your Black ass'll get offed wearing
   just about anyt—

> Church slacks? My short sleeve tee
   with "Black Achiever 2019" stitched
   across the ribs, and still no pass?

< *PASS* is a tenderheaded second line.
  PAST is a soft behind. This girl *PASSED*
  at the checkout. She had breath to breathe
  in the *PAST*. Get that? And from her backpack,
  police pulled panties, cream, a toothbrush . . .
  nothing orange. Nothing that belonged to
  the heifah holding the story.

> So regardless of our end, we don't get
  a *past*?

the unidentified skeletal remains of a black female

wearing a red Pringles Chip t-shirt, blue jeans, and white shoes   a red hooded jacket

Guess jacket, and a multi-colored scarf.   yellow sundress   sweats under the dress

a Bruins cap.

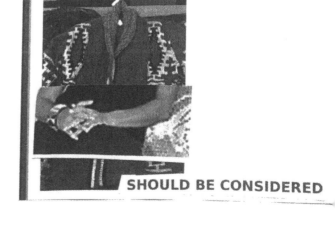

SHOULD BE CONSIDERED

Let Auntie tell it, I wasn't paying
no mind. But I heard every bit of that
murder she was skimming above my head.

Letitia?   Latoya?   something like that.

And when I found the name, fear had me
rip a switch from its yard. Fear had me
creased over a knee to be depleted.

I was mad.

Mad felt out of place like God   in a sitcom
or hair in a wound. But in the country of my hurt,
"mad" can mean "very much."

mad affected   mad offended   mad afflicted.

I was mad   in awe of all them eyes   on that Black girl's broke down life:

An issue with that Black girl, involving a right eye:

...ion. ...as ang...
...re...res bub... ...ace. There was the time, for example, that
she became irritated with her little sister and threw a fork at her from
across the kitchen table. It struck the girl in the right eye, causing per-
manent loss of sight.[167] Y... ...fe olor reve... ...ted ... ...and
resilience. Sh... was a ...

That Black girl, too fly in junior high with exotic eyes:

I used to tell her that I liked her cut [slanted] eyes.

. Everyone seemed to know her for her

...s."[173] Her...os...s...ch...

"Chinese eyes,"

...[174]...

And when that Black girl's name slipped a mind, "Chinese eyes" was harm moniker:

"I was at my locker
and this girl came up to me and said 'Latasha was killed.'

I said   who?

'Latasha,   you know
your best friend. The black girl with
the Chinese eyes,

Latasha!' }

24

A thin obsidian life is heaving
on a time limit you've set

Worst experiment of my life they are located at the cross
walk of Phoenix and 5th where lots of blacks live I just
went in there for hair and noticed I was being watched
thru mirrors in corners tho I go nowhere lookin broke
(I got jobS) but since I'm black this female just KNEW
I was gonna steal something right so I found the yaky
I wanted and went over to checkout where I asked this
heifer pointblank what her issue was and she gon say
some shit like "safety" I was hot y'all I said "I don't
need to take shit from here I got jobs PLURAL okay
and once the hood gets wind of your lil attitude this
hairstore gon go dark thru the windows forever, baby!"
No response. She didn't even bag my packs.
Won't be back.

Useful   Funny   Cool

INSTRUCTIONS: In this part, you will be given a list of statements regarding race and health. Some of these statements are true while others are not. Please consider each statement and rate the extent to which you believe it is true, from Definitely Untrue to Definitely True:

Whites, on average, have larger brains than Blacks.

⊙   I kept my eyes open when he   pierced my nose   just to prove I could

          watch this white man shoot me and   not blink once.

Black couples are significantly more fertile than White couples.

⊙   Each time Auntie pancaked a centipede to beige for scaring me,
she'd go   *Mean ol' centipede, you bleed like me!*   My embarrassment
still cringes. Serenading 'bout-to-be-ghosts seems a waste. A thin
obsidian life is heaving on a time limit you've set. Why sing at that?

Whites are less susceptible to heart diseases, like hypertension, than Blacks.

⊙   I thought septum piercings were African. I thought getting one
would make Lucky Dube an artery through my Saturdays. I survived
single-mother daughterhood, and for that I've earned the courage to
blast holes through my appearance. I've earned this bodily door.

Blacks are better at detecting movement than Whites.

⊙   There was a time when children made a sport of
        sprinting behind me on my dusk jogs. The
        winner was whoever caught up and slapped my
        ass first.   Once it happened right as I went to
        wrench my undies from the crack. Me and a
        blond brushed hands back there, right on
        the brilliant bluff of my brown sexuality.

Black people's nerve endings are less sensitive than White people's nerve endings.

⊙   Centipede is a delicacy, a sign of health in wider countries. But in the country
        of my hurt, a centipede can never be of help. I want badly for centipede to be a
        verb—to aggregate, to hone, to serenade the limit I've set.

Whites have more efficient respiratory systems than Blacks.

⊙   Auntie's favorite stereotype is *They're so violent!*—not methodically, but
        ad-libish; a think-on-your-feet-type knockout. Though I've never gone
        to blows, she hopes that within me, somewhere along the carotid, my African
        American inadequacy could shiv its acrylics into power.

Black people's skin has more collagen (i.e. it's thicker) than White people's skin.

⊙   I wasn't mad enough to violence the children. Sometimes, if I ran
        earplugged and vinyl-layered, I couldn't feel the winner make a finish line
        of me at all.

SHOULD BE CONSIDERED

that Black women's dreams continue to put a run
in the tights of colonial rule. In war,
these women are taken into theaters, tanks, and
pueblos, and in these places they are harmed
to harm their countries.

Black women are a point that's made.

air in a variety of styles and dress in African tribal clothing.

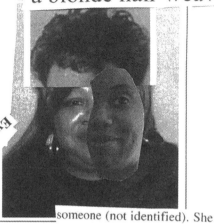

a blonde hair weave.

Eyes:

Unknown

a scar under her right eye

red/white/blue Nikes, and may also be

someone (not identified). She

No clothing was located in the area

was last seen wearing light

ROZEAL
Untitled (after Kikugawa Eizan's
"Furyu nana komachi"
[The Modern Seven Komashi])
2007
Acrylic and paper on panel

BUBBLE SISTERS
"Bubble Song"
Album: Bubble Sisters
Universal Music Korea
2003
Music Video

Sounds like a docent says
indium-style, so we sit electric on a
birch church pew facing
a no-title painting.

Bubble Sisters sing their single
on a yellow club stage. A three-minute
performance beneath god and
a seesaw of light. I'm

Untitled: portrait of a woman with blue
view, bleach cornrows ending in a Sly Stone fro,
ten Tabasco acrylics.

in a funk over braids, nails, rollers, fros,
Bantu knots. I'm mad at all four of their faces,
cork-dye alive.

She looks white to me, but her mug is
slightly vandalized with the color I am.

An act of blackface well-intended,
giving the finger to Eurocentric beauty.

A placard to the left names the concept—
Ganguro: Japanese fashion.
Girls wearing dark foundation, faux nails,
tresses teased to the touch of fleece

Minstrelsy setting out to prove that K-pop
stars could be unconventional
with conviction, that K-pop stars could be
unfair, unaware, unthin, unthem, but

When the artist came across ganguro, her opinion of it wore a deep side part:

thoroughly talonted. Could be anti-stunning and stun. Could starshine and be clay nieces of mine.

On one side, she was satisfied by this international Black fascination. Tho

Over here, we sho do go oops upside the head of any mocking fashion nations.

on the other, every faux loc left in fascination seemed lye-relaxed and flaccid, lil tassel in the national rearview.

When fascination perms kitchens and coons for bruises, when it makes scantrons of paper bags, the nigga delegation better ask why u feel a need to do that?

Why the darkening of skin, she asked? Why do they feel the need to do that? I had to do something to figure out what I thought. I'm still not sure I know what I think.

Why that dank fit and drama skit? Why you feel the need to do us? We gotta do somethin' quick to flaunt what we threat. We still unnerved and unsure, picking at that scab over what we think.

CONSIDER that our ansisters have incredible side eye—the talent of seeing things they are not directly looking at; an adaptation from lynchings, beatings and other fearings. Consider they were convinced into colonies, corsets, boycotts, jobs and, in these robberies, were harmed to harm a concept.

Spooked by a slew of layoffs, I bought a mini marquee to slouch against the top shelf of my cubicle. That sign was my first tactic to stand out in a slave's place without directly standing, jiving, or smiling, as I hated doing those in war zones during the week. A second tactic was my wardrobe choice on Wednesdays, the days of our staff meeting. I took the little kiki as an opportunity to dress a way that roused a pubic interest: kente cloths, ankh socks, Bantu knots—I was partial to the emblems of elders. Senegalese twists, 4C yaki ponies on a bungee drawstring—dark and gaudy, I felt I could not be removed.

I spent weekends perusing the ruins of hoods, sticks, and boonies in pursuit of clothing as foreign and unrelatable as possible. Some were holey and needed sewing or would sag so needed shrinking on high heat dry, as I was, at the time, losing weight to be familiar and relatable as possible.

My mini marquee posed the question, *What r u pretending not to know 2day?* A coworker sent me:

Sweetie, that sign!   Best,

Yes! Ms. Toni Cade Bambara.   Cheers,

Moorison?   Best,

*Morrison? No. Toni of Queens, the
obscene of Bed-Stuy.   Cheers,

She wrote about that milkman, right? Black
and breastfed too long. Best,

This the Toni of deep sightings; of guerilla
love and cheers,

In the passed, I've been even worse with first
names. Now I probably got Cade twisting in some
dirty borough's grave. ☹   Best,

Passed is a tenderheaded second line.
Past, a soft behind. Toni *PASSED* in some
December. You called me Keisha in the
PAST, remember? And if any Black woman
turned an inch in any grave, you'd feel Ares
wait the Woolworth counters 'tween the
pleats of police jeeps. Gods like Toni, I don't
ever remember them waiting.

Cheers,

FALSE

According to magazine polls, the three things Black women fear most are dogs, ghosts, and CCTV.

CONTEXT:

Two magazines
Country Living (99.99% white readership)
and *EBONY/JET* (99.99% black readership)
held surveys to see what their readers fear most.

Country Living's top responses were
1. Nuclear war in US
2. Child dying of terminal illness
3. Terminal illness of self

EBONY/JET's were
1. Dogs
2. Ghosts
3. CCTV

ORIGIN:

Stereotypes are centipedes at ease
in bowls of bleach. Or liberation lit

with wicks, and then Katrina—that's
a stereotype. When company's mixed, I'll pet

king shepherds, adore mausoleums, suck my
teeth in corner store camcorders, although

privately—under nouveau R&B and the tutelage of
quick weaves—the Chesimard in me counts horror on

a matte black abacus. There is no fear on
earth that has ever gone unhad or

unbereaved, but the Diaspora won't have it be
known that dogs, ghosts, and CCTV are

a melody defining our costs, copywriting our loss.
I'm scared of saying what I'm tryna say. I'm saying

I'm a ghetto-scared future   beautiful
and Beauty is what gets hardshipped,

mishandled. What arrives overnight, over-
weight. What was unleashed from hoses onto Hosea

Williams. What voted for tax cuts and sleep.
As a twenty-four-year-old perishable

feud item, how can I not fear cop mutts bucking at
me in lethal language? Problem being

I'm Bebe's kids with scissors when it comes to
English. I'm scared to say what I came

alive to say, spooked my head will expire
before my so-deserving Black ass can be worked

into a purpose worth some acres
and a heartbeat. Most noons, I beg Orisha

Oya to undread my scared, to sop up
my mourning with hot gauze although

I'll miss my washrags stiff
with soap, my stomach slick with

SunnyD and stage-frightened mariposas.
I'll miss dancing flat—roadkill-flat—the plush

yams of my Black

insecurity. Eyebrows like two jet burns above
sight and all night a Sagittarian Toni

sitting in my throat, dog-earing Zane,
Kool-Aiding the cookout, coating her tits with

shea, her cussing breath with citrus so that dogs,
ghosts, and CCTV can be—what should I call it—

a *grove* in me?

The phenomenon of withholding

★ ☆ ☆ ☆ ☆

Racist.

We ate at a bfast food truck parked across the way. I had
too much juice and of course there were no restrooms,
so I walked across the street to this braiding salon, hoping
to use theirs. When I got inside, they told me there were
no restrooms to use. "None. At. All."

Mind you, my two friends had gone to this exact same
salon just 15 minutes prior and were allowed to use the
restrooms: no eye rolling, no teeth sucking, no questions.

So I asked these ladies why my friends had been allowed
to use their restroom but I wasn't. They just shrugged and
scrunched their eyebrows up at me like they had no clue
what I was saying.

I'm Asian. My two friends are white.

It should be considered.

Useful   Funny   Cool

I TUTOR in the Center for Writing and Speaking. My job is to lend an editorial hand. The work consists of two-hour shifts four days a week during which I situate in a room bordered with the blooms and cows of O'Keefe.

I get $11.50 for every hour my assistance lasts. If someone especially likes my help, they'll arrange a weekly session. I meet a certain student Wednesdays on a loveseat beneath *Black Iris*. Our mother languages make these sessions a tetris. For the tutee, I suspect, I'm an oddly dark reminder of the English and the eagle left to earn.

I've been detrimentally molded for my role here. Ebonic nicks on my tongue took long walks down rank MLK pkwys so that I could shuffle like Cupid through some beneficial hinges. As a tutor, my job is to initiate that same vernacular evacuation in others.

At our seventh session, I review an essay in which the prompt instructs her to *write about a time when you experienced culture shock, the feeling of displacement, discomfort, or uneasiness when entering a new society or way of life.* She writes that while living in South Korea her perception of America was tutored by television: white chicks sprawled like used parachutes on the hoteled coasts of Californian beaches. I think, *maybe* Laguna Beach *or* Baywatch? Then men in the states—rock stars sharpened by Percocet and leather, incorrect presidents or fragile average joes—I think, *maybe DiCaprio or Cusack, the beau of* Say Anything?

But when my tutee arrived, she did not arrive on a beach or DC's Foggy Bottom. Compton: all naked of glamour and skyscraper. The Southside, cockeyed, cockamamie, off-center, off-white.

"When I arrived, I was disappointed."

Where was white bay, white buck, white belt, white rot, white hope, white cells, the White House . . .

"I did not know there would be so many   black people here."

. . . white trash, white wash, white ways, white flight, white knight, white chip, white chocolate?

"I was disappointed to see so many   people here."
                                                        black

hampton

honolulu

cotton

cane

plaçage myth

picture brides

lynchings

linnaeus

dragon lady

sapphire

the yellow man and the girl

the birth of a nation

d. r. millard

j. m. sims

bootstraplessness

I see our disappointments begin

          at the crux of   people's involvement.
               white

los angeles county

south central

the valley

loiterer

merchant

free huey

yellow peril supports black power

menace

menaced

riots

sa-i-gu

the los angeles black-korean alliance

black lives matter

asian american letters for black lives

A TIMELINE DETAILS A SERIOUSNESS of events. As a diagram of occurrence, a timeline's chief objective is to show how passed happenings caution and contaminate our contemporary sense of momentum. A professor may author timelines to teach what precedes and follows genocide. On the overhead, Rwanda is a centipede with its head in Belgium and tail on stage of the '05 Oscars. In our text, the Bodo League Massacre is an annotated string I spill grits on to suffocate the start, the blood count, the South. Easing on down the Eastern Hemisphere's lines of time, the decline of nonwhite worlds may fervently thaw on me. It may dawn on ya girl with a hyper sense of tension that democracy is a phenomenon of withholding things: crossing legs, clenching assholes, silencing radios, pinning lips.

But rather than events, I want timelines to detail a sermon of interactions. On my tutee's line would be interactions had with Hollywood and, so, interactions had with the American art of erasure. Likewise, on my timeline, interactions with Aunt Notrie and, so, interactions with retail. Between her knees, I received cowrie cornrows and corner store warnings— tales of 'iquas and 'ishas entering shops without sensation: hands out their pockets, hands off the shelves, hands to the heaven-high fluorescents. Girls who knew what to buy before going inside *'cause we don't survive the browsing*. Between Auntie's knees, I shop while Black. I interact with racism without having to have its truncheons twerk the roof of my mood quite yet. My interactions with that imminent ism, secondhand.

So I'm drawing a line. On it, each tick mark represents an interaction Latasha Harlins and Soon Ja Du had with Empire Liquor Market through the experience of someone else. Secondhand horrors, all before the bell above the door snitched to mention their entrance on March 16, 1991.

Direct your heartbreak to a tick representing Latasha's uncle Richard, who manned Empire's register in June of 1990. Latasha, having interacted with her uncle, must have interacted with his working hardship: he was hawk-watched on shifts, monitored on trips to the restroom. One day, Mr. Du even demanded he work overtime without pay: "You supposed to

work for free. Do what black people are
supposed to do."

Unc says avoid them spots that stalk with mirrors and feet.
Latasha could avoid some stalkings, but avoid them all?
Avoiding them all could mean a mean vitamin C deficiency.

oreo	
	twinkie
coolest monkey in the jungle	
	wong brothers. a laundry service. 555-wong. two wongs can make it white. abercrombie & fitch.
click for ebony babes!	
	hot asians awake in your area!
pusha	
	phd
welfare	
	well-mannered
. . . all have AIDS	
	chinavirus
you're living in poverty, your schools are no good, you have no jobs, 58 percent of your youth is unemployed. what the hell do you have to lose?	
	bootstraps

THOUGH OUR PROFESSOR SAYS Hutu and Tutsi were societies prior to colonialism, timelines say Belgium made these divisions ethnic, relegating Tutsis to aristocracy and seven-seater limousines. Though our professor claims that after WWII our troops assist with Korea's independence, timelines emphasize occupation as Seoul's intro to jumping Jim Crow—*souljas* steeping beans for *soldiers* bibbed to eat.

Timelines prove the origin of race is oral storytelling. For race to work, man must tell a story that the fools recite forever.

Aunt Notrie read me *The Bluest Eye*, *Imitation of Life*, a thin novella called *Passing*—in it, a woman named Clare inherits no pigment. She's perceived as white, so sidesteps the memoir of Blackness altogether. This comes to matter in her manner of marriage, of capital, dress, and revival. A similar mistake could've saved Latasha at the counter or Renisha at the screen, Breonna in the sleep. For Black to work, race must tell a story wherein Hutu are dung, wherein Han Hyun-min is dirt. For Blackness to work, Black people must be forbidden to leave it. Forced back in its shroud, Clare takes, or is made to take, a final step to shed it. For such a step to work, someone had to leave this arena to the fools.

So on my timeline, I'll tell the foolish stories Soon Ja inherits: before being Empire's shopkeeper, she interacts with the store solely through the cautions of her man—his accounts of absent police, racial slurs, Crip threats, robberies, petty thefts at the acrylic tips of 'iquas and 'ishas.

Soon Ja inherits his horror of Black interaction   a fear that, one night in '90, wrongs a life:

A Black man witnesses a driveby.   He runs into Empire for refuge.   Out of fear,
Mr. Du forces him

back on the block.   Brotha is shot
in the head.

Ion kno *why* you tryna **act** like you cleaning up.

Hurry **up and** buy.

This ain't Korea, China, or **wherever you**
come from. You get some Miller High life
in **this** fuckin' joint.

Just pay and **leave**.

Gon'head get me **that Olde** E.

You buy another beer.

Ay, why'on you give my **home**boy his change?

You are not to drink beer in **store**.

Can't stand y'all **motherfuckers**.

I feel sorry for your mother.

When **we get through** fuckin' with these
Koreans, me **and** you **go to** Roscoe's Chicken 'n'
Waffles----on me.

Hurry up and **go**!

What you say about my **mama**?

I don't **want** any **trouble**. Just get out.

Either them Korean **motherfuckers are** genius
or your **black**asses just plain dumb.

Trouble just **get** out.

It was funny like that   in the **hood sometimes.**

We could avoid each other.   We could avoid events that breed a white supremacy between us. But whiteness is intrinsic to all transactions in this country. Avoiding white power means passing away.

Four memorials

I'm not kidding when I say every time I go to Numero
Uno, I get racially profiled. They don't even have the decency
to be slick about it. I thought I was overreacting at first or being
sensitive because I'm Black, but it's clearly a pattern. I even
tested my theory by going to another Numero Uno and,
you guessed it, I got the SAME CRIMINAL TREATMENT.
Almost to a T. Almost like they get together and rehearse this
at the staff meeting. This is business as usual. This is how it
goes for Black folks. And seeing as this was where Latasha
Harlins was shot, it's a real shame nothing's changed.

I say close it down. Make it a shelter or a museum, something
worth something.

Useful   Funny   Cool

1:

While writing *Concentrate*, I was often nagged by the haint of reluctance. It was driven by an insecurity surrounding my lack of proximity to the subject—I was writing about a city I'd never been to, fumes I hadn't witnessed, a span of years in which I wasn't even thought of yet. *Girl*, reluctance said, *all you got is secondhand.*

So I head to LA to handle the archive, to stand at the foot of every place I talk up, to earn the facts and their phantoms firsthand.

The epicenter of my curiosity is 91st and Figueroa, the lot on which Empire Liquor Market stood. Empire: a collection of states under one dominion; omnipotent premises; a territory implying power and power implying those who die in the course of courting it.

On 91st and Figueroa stood a structure, a system akin to a kingdom.

Business never resumed after Latasha was killed inside. Vacancy made it a feasible target. On the first night of revolution, there were several attempts to incinerate it. But Black residents living next door at the Webb Motel stayed up into the wee hours, filling garbage cans with water. Living so close by, barely two feet from the store, they knew the fate of Empire would have also been the fate of their home. To save their own lives, they had to save this monument of brutality. Our survival, inextricable from the structures that threaten it.

In the late 1990s, Empire's signage was peeled from the building and replaced with that of Numero Uno Market. This is the face that greets me now.

Unlike the stone-white dress of its predecessor, Numero is a pink and green shock to the street. I see a parking lot and a threshold in the back where trucks relieve themselves of cereal, seafood, juice. Inside, three officers linger by the liter sodas. I watch a butcher conceive slivers of meat. A child walks aisles freely, motherless, unhesitant. I make efforts to push my shoulders back but hesitate. I grab a grocery bag, eager for artifact. I hover at the refrigerators, eyeing a camera above the door. I walk around, consumed by questions of configuration. Is everything in the same place? Is this where Soon Ja tended the counter, a gun her clandestine companion? Evidence takes imagination now.

But those who love Latasha do imagine. In 2016, on the twenty-fifth anniversary of her loss, photos slouched against this edifice. Balloons ascended by the fence, dressing the hood in cool helium. On the sidewalk, a pastor prayed for protection, for wherewithal, for a heaven-eyed CCTV.

Numero's sidewalk was also the location for an interview with Latasha's aunt, Denise Harlins. Denise helped raise Latasha, a duty assumed in her twenties after Latasha's mother was murdered in a nightclub. Denise took over the role of hair and heart care. Like many Black women, Denise found herself swept into a motherhood necessitated by grief.

The interviewer asked Denise if she ever got the chance to see Soon Ja Du in the flesh. I watch auntie look up and off camera, ushering in that memory:

> "Oh yeah, I saw her . . . I went to court. Was only one day I missed court and that day I had to—that night—I had to go to the hospital 'cause both my glands were swole up so bad, 'cause I was out here doing the work, I ain't gon' lie to you."

The work of petitions, politicians, protests, and, on the first night of uprising, assisting the Webb Motel—Denise hoped to transform Empire into a center of excellence for South Central children.

All of her work, a resistance. And such resistance menaces the body. In resistance, we are at the neck of injustice, holding our breath, proving our matter. Resistance antagonizes immunity, makes us prone to roadrunner pulse. Epidemiologist Sherman A. James calls this "John Henryism," theorizing that the tireless effort required to combat racial injustice has a direct correlation to the prevalence of hypertension in Black communities.

Aunt Denise died of congestive heart failure.

You'd be a fool to assume the work of resistance had no part, no say, no hand.

Denise continued,

"The day of the hearing—and it was probably divine
intervention—my glands were so swole I couldn't go
to court.   And I seen it on TV.   And when
the verdict came back, I fell   on my knees, and I
just shouted to my highest   high, and I

was angry.

I knew the fix was in then . . .

I knew the fix was in then."

But there are no signs of murder, memorial, or resistance when I arrive. The ground is like any ground. Normalcy devastates. Stillness lies to me about history.

At the scene, The Angels PD urge Mr Du   *sir, lower your hand!*   During the death, Mr. Du was asleep in the family van. The bark of the shot, the snitch of surveillance, it conceives Ali butterfly-bee under which Soon Ja dissolves. Knuckles were no foreign performance in their marriage. In mine, wifebeaters yank back my wigcaps all the time. Above each assault, White Jesus lit His loosie and I became the cameraman involved. All I could think was Ellis the island and mammie the mast, a ton in our shooting deaths. Blood orange and blood of baby girl whiffed up from the sill, both swearing in patois and smelling lilac-good. But then, Jesus ashed His cig and clocked outta His shift. He no longer needed women of color to make His point about obedience; He had mammograms and Candy Man for that. A city's number one killer of people is people who are obedient to their senses. Sense outlawed—now wouldn't that be trife? Jesus would need us so pathetically then! But in any life, it's never my business why the savior is the color of a wedding dress and not tap shoes. I'll have my book of light and He'll have His. For killing anyone, He and mammograms have their lofty reasons and our men have theirs, tenderized as they are. But any afterlife—a Paradise—is no killer of colored girls even when pushed. The skies of that sort of nirvana are innocent and inconsolable as we laze forward, inventing simultaneous gods to save us. Ornery gods of pansex, midterms, safe medications. We create gods without histories, without which they are made only of air and belief. No punishment.

2:

Bret Harte Prep is a beige row of rectangles on South Hoover Street, a nine-minute walk from Numero Uno. Latasha learned here from 1988 to 1990.

At the entrance, a man sits in a folding chair and a woman stands farther back under the hood of the walkway. Every now and then, her pacing brings her nearer the daylight, nearer my knowing. From what I can tell, this pair has the task of welcoming students inside, checking their names against a clipboard list—a pandemic protocol, protection measure.

I won't disrupt the flow of operations. I came to meet the building, read the marquee's bold announcements, see that bird up on the roof. Disturbed by the scent of my investigation, she leaves.

I admire the pavement textured with language, script left by those who passed as the sidewalk dried into permanence. This is how we commemorate—graffiti on the scalps of trains, the lower waists of offices, sharpies to a bathroom stall, twigs ushered through newborn concrete. All of it, our way of reclaiming the narrative of a place, leaving a mark that costs the state money to eradicate.

I read the scratches down South Hoover and back: "BAby," "Vicious," "4loc H-WOOD," "HOLLY," "MIKE," "DARRY," "MAShAWN," "Westly," "Dip," "ALEX III," "JEROME SMITH," then, the name I came here for.

I'm encouraged by how Latasha lasts at the door of her education. Someone, maybe even a child who attends Bret Harte now, knew enough to cut her name in an irreversible place. Perhaps this child sat between the knees of an auntie who conjured the name with one command: *Don't forget it*. I'm encouraged because, as the saying goes, we live only as long as the memories of others. Black people, as a means of survival, have endeavored to keep long memories.

I didn't plan on talking. I didn't wanna bother nobody, but there's a sudden volume in my relief. So I seek that woman at the entrance. I ask if there are any tributes or plaques or mentions of Latasha at all inside the school.

When Latasha's name leaves my mouth, the woman's face presents the problem. It's the look an accidental wound gives its random, careless maker. I feel it before she says it—a grave has entered our interaction.

"Who?"

Latasha Lavon Harlins, ma'am. Born Capricorn, born cornered. Known for walking in an Empire and never walking out. This horror was first told to me when I entered my body, so as I settle in unsettling skin, I book a room inside her absence. A room of no light and all lore but I've entered, a fool, to find her. I've entered like Alice Walker in Eatonville for Zora Neale, coming to raise her, name her saint. Just like that, I've entered LA to anti-erase, which is a work of resistance. The absent can only live in memory. As the saying goes, if you disremember us, you kill us, and I'm here to resist a second dying. I need you to know this was Latasha's school, and now her name is a wound in its sidewalk.

Flyers on Slauson Avenue have a photo of Soon Ja Du and claim THIS WOMAN OWNS BUDDHA MARKET. SHOP AT YOUR OWN RISK! The flyers pose in Buddha's windowsill and arrive at checkout to work the nerve or end the work of baby girl's killer. But the owner of Buddha Market waves a legal page divulging her name—Annie Shin. *Who?* Annie. Owner of Buddha on Slauson Avenue. Not Soon Ja Du. Du is free, moved to the Valley. She ain't around the hood to work the nerve of now. At checkout, you scream **up** the breast of Annie Shin. You Minute Maid her blouses. When you bang on Buddha's counter, you unbless the boats of an entire people. We the people really somethin' else. Our anger is the valley and guess who lives there now. Exhume a name to drag it through enlightenment past the Swishers, past the liq, and guess that cost. Guess who owes it now.

3:

On my way to the Algin Sutton Recreation Center, I take in Vermont Vista: Barbary fig in a front yard, the Virgin Mary taped against a window. Two men chatting in lawn chairs on a driveway, a clothesline flaunting mauve sheets behind them.

It's quiet, foreign to my assumptions, which are all tutored by television.

The mural text reads:

WE
QUEENS

I am very reliable
and trustworthy
honest.
I have a lot of
talent, and I know
whatever I set my
mind on something
I can accomplish
I show people I care by
giving what I have
to people who
actually need it.

Latasha Lavon Harlins
January 1, 1976 – March 16, 1991

I'm at the rec center to view a mural of Latasha. Artist Victoria Cassinova painted it on the building's side face in early 2021. The color, still young. I rub its hem, half-expecting to draw back a rich hand. The only section segregated from the palette are three small doves tarrying off to the right of Latasha's head, their flight defined in sobering grayscale.

Here, I learn Latasha was a poet. Opposite the doves, Cassinova transcribed a poem of Latasha's written a month before her death.

Her piece is reminiscent of an "I am" poem I wrote in grade school. I was given "I am _____" and asked to fill in the blank ten times or so. Often, I switched "I am" for stronger leads: I wonder _____. I hear _____. I see _____. I pretend _____. I dream _____.

A Celebration of Young Poets – Wisconsin Spring 2004

I Am

ird
frog
ies

I am a beautiful girl who is scared of what may happen in the future
I wonder if dolls move or talk when you're not looking
I hear nature's cry
I see the ship going to the Bahamas
I want my family to never get sick
I am a beautiful girl who is scared of what may happen in the future
I pretend to be characters in movies

ex Bathe
School
enosha
rade 4

I feel tornados are scary
I touch the ocean's bank
I worry that there will not be enough room for people on the earth in the future
I cry during sad movies
I am a beautiful girl who is scared of what may happen in the future
I understand that everything doesn't go your way
I say treat blacks the same as you would treat whites
I dream that the world was perfect
I try to be successful in school

net

I hope my mother will live a long and healthy life
I am a beautiful girl who is scared of what may happen in the future

Hinds
School
lington

Courtney Taylor
Wilson Elementary School
Mequon
Grade 5

My poem, maimed by fear of catastrophe, of breath in the inanimate, unbridled anxiety. But in Latasha's work, there's uninterrupted possibility. Reading her lines, I bear witness to how a Black girl once spoke life into herself:

I have a lot of / talent, she writes.

Latasha could dance, which earned her a spot on the Algin Sutton drill team. Her favorite artist was Bell Biv DeVoe, and so, when I imagine her moves, I imagine them scored by new jack.

I care by / giving what I have / to people who / actually need it

Latasha wanted to study law, a dream had in the aftermath of her mother's murder. Latasha understood there to be a world of women nonwhite and wounded, a world of mothers refused long, healthy lives. She recognized there to be a world lacking people who cared about this, people unwilling to give what they have.

I am very reliable / and trustworthy

That word—*trust*. It pops me in the mouth. Soon Ja's lack of trust is the cause of this mural, the impetus for our public display of memory. But as I see here, trust was something Latasha had already affirmed in herself. Her trustworthiness on March 16, 1991, was fact.

4:

Some yards behind the mural sits the playground where Latasha spent much of her youth. That too is bestowed with her name now.

A child's murder leaves a hypertrophic scar on the place where it happens. Councilmember Marqueece Harris-Dawson affirmed this at the playground's unveiling: "Mississippi has Emmett Till. Florida's got Trayvon Martin. Los Angeles has Latasha Harlins."

Now whenever the babies of Vermont Vista climb and swing and slide, they will be doing so in the scarred lap of legacy. A child may ask, "Who?" The adults will answer however they do, but their answers will irritate history.

I'm lifted by the mural and the playground, but Algin Sutton is a haunted home for them. It is both Latasha's adolescent sanctuary and her inauguration into abuse, the place where she was pursued by a counselor twice her age. Jerry was a source of argument in the Harlins household. *So you think you grown? You think you in love?*

I care by / giving, she writes.

Rape is a room within every cishet man. It's either locked or onerously doorless. There's no hotline there, no soap. On the nightstand, a lobbyist kills the age of permission. In the armoire, a god nears the end of its utility. Outside, a chauffeur waits to escort us to the curb of our murders. An auntie is driven nieceless.

I show people I care by / giving what I have

Aunt Denise pulls up to the rec in '91 to begin resistance. Her message to this nigga is quite simple: *Stop touching my child*. When she exits, he's left with eavesdropping colleagues, and his next move is to disprove. He calls Denise a drunk, says she's clearly out her mind: *Don't nobody know what she talking 'bout. Don't nobody want nothing to do with no girl.*

So don't nobody in the rec center make a report. Don't nobody in the rec keep an eye on Latasha. Don't nobody in the rec protect this baby. Jerry continues his violence until there is no more Latasha to violence. Don't nobody consider her a baby?

I know / whatever I set my / mind on something / I can accomplish / I show people

Men like Jerry get away with murder because their murders are of the innocent. Innocence is a fact you must believe in to save. Innocence is a fact we'll need a warrant to touch.

Everything that I've ever done
I keep in a jar marked *innocent*
so that men can't touch it.

Most flies tire of gossip
they've prayed to be on the wall of.
They roll such funky eyes, yawning

over grownfolks' most beautiful
business. I sit with hands tied in a lie
behind my own ass, a patient

afro donkey. I am the only trick alive
and with eyes who likes outgrown
acrylics and who likes it when

wind blows a water fountain's show
onto a sidewalk in a park the size
of Paradise. I think, *righteous confetti*. Yesterday

I am twenty-six and the home
he will rape me in has not been
built yet. Catching my fat reflection

in an hourglass, I don't seem capable
of creating what I have: a fear with proportions
the size of disaster. Paradise and disaster

are the exact same size for me. My fear
is a park and inside of her a water
fountain blows its show onto

styrofoam boardwalks. The house
she'll find me trippin' in has not
been built, yet it's gorgeous and owned

by men who touch jars
marked *capable*. I know facts about
ancient Troy and one popular myth

about Trojans: *If u carry one,*
u won't need it. If u leave it,
u'll seem clean or

childishly kind.   I kill a fly minding its business
on a sidewalk inside of me today. Why?   I know I'll enjoy
the music. As a mother of something Black, I owe flies

nothing. Nothing. I owe
nothing. Remember that.

Citrus visiting me with cruelty

I'm browsing satin caps . . . he's on my neck.
I'm holding packs of FreeTress . . . he's stacking
combs on the wrong rack. I'm checking the wall
of wigs . . . he's sweeping the floor between my feet.
Avoid this store, ladies. The man who owns it will
reduce you everywhere.

Useful Funny Cool

Latasha may've spent her last night of
life with Jerry, that counselor from the
rec. I take the news of this tough
as tit, hard as whipped
LeVar, but shit, let that had been me—Aunt Notrie
at home, *VIBE* magazine funneled to a gnat swatter
on her lap, hair bonnet knotted and nails half-periwinkle-
wet—she would've popped outta bed and steered the Buick with
knees if it meant snatching me, her tried-true maneuver
to save me. But without Black mamas on the night-
shift of our lives, many of our eyes on
men go lilac with that tiny pink bow on the sternum of
our undershirts missing. Having, in the nick of time,
survived a man's one bed, I do admit turning my
pelvis to begin it. Since everything that has a beginning
must have an end, I let my assault begin so that it would end.
I was at his all-white Nikes with bleach and an Oral-B
when I found a VHS called *Can't We All Just
Get It On?* flattening some drugstore honey
buns. I had agreed to watch it, but had
agreed to nothing else.

In the early 1870s, at the mouth of the Big Bend Tunnel, John Henry beat a mechanical steam drill in a "steel driving" contest. Moments after, he dropped dead from complete physical and mental exhaustion.

⊙   He knew the brunch specials by heart. He knew the OJ needed three sugars without sipping it first. I go, "Can't we enjoy new foods together? Why take me someplace you've already eaten?"

The John Henryism hypothesis assumes that African Americans are routinely exposed to psychosocial stressors (eg., financial strain, job insecurity, and social insults linked to race or social class) that require considerable energy each day to manage.

⊙   Watching suburban insecurities perforate another Keisha on FOX 5, we notice bedazzled apples on her cadaver jean butt. I go, "Apple Bottom in 2022? Where her fur boots at?" He spews Heineken down the duvet, and I consider how our denim statistically outlives its buyer while, it's probable, Levi Strauss and Brooks Brothers don't face this bloodswag likelihood.

John Henryism is measured by a participant's level of agreement with the following statements:

(1) I've always felt that I could make of my life pretty much what I wanted to make of it.

⊙   He keep looking for receipts. He wanna see the female I'm being during the week.   Could my baby be born with that?

(2) Once I make up my mind to something, I stay with it until the job is completely done.

⊙   In a second nightmare, I deliberately call all my dirt night skies off,
hush my ovaries into a bowtie—wall-to-wall starshine. In it, I'm a new
Keisha blowing the sergeant, miming *schadenfreude!* in his nooses.
Last thing I do is lemon the lesion, citrus visiting me with cruelty.

(3) I like doing things that other people thought could not be done.

⊙   Fructose is addictive, so I might be in trouble. Not that I necessarily crave it, but when
it's available I don't deprive my taste. At the OB clinic, they swab my sense then
mention the blues, though I tenant the same sick hood as you. How's your blood
taking sugar with such sportsmanship?

(4) When things don't go the way I want them to, that just makes me work even harder.

⊙   What I meant was   could my baby be born   with that tension?

After Toyin Salau, I called everyone with a difficult life
in my life.

Gaslight. Before 2016, I had not heard of it.

                  Breakfast is severed. Sunny-side up eggs, little
                  water beds. Clover honey flooding up the
                  forehead of a bear. Kettle finna cry while
                     his piss rings porcelain behind
                            the only door in our apartment—

but after he hit me, doors between us
were over.

Aaliyah died in the section of me
that stinks—the cortex, where all
my African American inadequacies meet
to make a yam-textured memory. Surely,
my grind pales compared to her *work*
of the middle, but that chart topper had
my preteen middle sofa-pinned and
dredging up, too often, a caramelized zeal
in marksmen. In men like my ex, Darnell,
who can't legally touch the sod of any school
yard; or R. Kelly, who's southern now,
stepping on the surname of peachtrees.　　　Sis, as a village
we need to want electric chairs when
it's right. Let's agree that every brotha's
obsession with what's juvenile is
filthy, that it fuels and shapes a fellating
power, which is the sort of power we fold,
sweep, and bleach way too
gladly. I heard Aaliyah check a male
reporter once:　*I'm AH-liyah,　like ah-men or Muhammad Ah-li,*
　　　　never UH-liyah　like uh-mazed or
　　　　uh-praise.　　Let's not desert our names
for ease of journalism either. My full name is
my mother's sole crack at poetry and here
I am, privileged to haul it like a tax
bracket or a satchel of proof.

Say we condensed Jerry's rape to fit inside
the archive. Clearly there'd be a scale issue.
So leave it out on 91st. We'll have it work
where as a college tutor I shoo a leaf
from its hood and a docent offers up
the number of autumns my abuser deserved
to miss—*if only you had given his name to
nametakers!* Blue Tupperware still makes
Russian dolls in the cabinet above the sink where
I sprawled for relaxers, where Auntie rinsed cough
syrup cups, snap peas, and soon I'll doll my daughter in
loose jeans with no forgiveness. I'll swear to her that
at first in life there will be no touching. Life will
kick off like curfew at a bougie mall and during her
hard menarche, the Holy Ghost will shout like
sneezes in a hand. Guilt will whoop the habitat
behind every Black man's head and to his crimes
we'll be ret to say, *You tried to kill me but
you missed. Now who's the master
of what happened?*

CONSIDER that Crystal Harlins, mama of Latasha Harlins, put restraining orders out on her man but men don't rest. She and her baby share a manner of death. Motherless, Latasha cries when in any car that rides beside a gumline of graves. It is hard. It is harm to ride beside the scenes of men's responsibility.

CONSIDER that Soon Ja assembled couches to fund her husband's dream of convenience, that she did so while inhabiting a woman's place: cinched sheets, such flawless boxes in the armoire, three babies fed a tenuous milk, and all the days he wanted sex, he got sex all the days he wanted it.

SHOULD BE CONSIDERED

that millard made double eyelids

rehearsing the trick on you

we are harmed

that sims made vicious, speculums

dismantling sis like explosives

to soothe a master

CONSIDER

that now I'm in a nigga with no answers, disturbed. I cover my drink, fist my Saab keys, check the backseat— a curriculum to groom the echoes. Downtown, my rape kit collector takes a sip of water and so my whole life takes a sip of that water.

SHOULD BE CONSIDERED that backhands in the homes of our descendants are statistically unlikely to lower. At the precinct, our pussies and eyelids give fingerprints and Linnaeus takes a sip of gaslight.

CONSIDER that safety measures between us, like restraining orders and doors, were invented to convince . . .

Concentrate. We have decisions to make.

Fire is that decision to make.

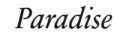

★ ★ ☆ ☆ ☆

BLACK OWNED BUT HOURS WRONG ONLINE,   WASTED A TANK &
MY TIME,   GOT THERE,   DOOR LOCKED,   LOOKED INSIDE, BLACK
INSIDE,   CALLED NEXT DAY, OWNER NASTY,   HUNGUP ON ME!

I will find a Korean store.

Useful   Funny   Cool

Aunt Notrie died in the t-shirt & tummy of
the man in the middle of America;~ was cervical, o-
varian? one of the southern cancers;~ like the last

blast of eczema, she left a considerable
itch in her dying;~ obese grief nursed on me
like a satin leech;~ xanax, a holy host, a

nimble quilt;~ her favorite color

was silk, which was not also her
favorite feeling;~ thank the Black redeemer
it was me;~ urine running

clear for weeks;~ snatching a fist-
ful of denim to uproot a cameltoe but
with it coming the bush unburning;~ being

colored is cooling hands down the sweats

of OJs;~ it is, with Raid, watching
roaches undergo an entertaining
petrifaction;~ learning how one strand of my

kinks & a pride of centipedes
curl close when they *just*
through, honey;~ this finality, finally

I welcome it—its lucid birth, litigious
burst;~ Aunt Notrie died in me like some
withered Dooney & Bourke, like

the burnt rind of a lemon;~ life-insured but
"daughter of Shango" was / is her most
preexisting condition;~ seven years

ago today, my stretch marks made the laugh lines

of a leftist markswoman;~ my hips, two white
liars;~ y'all 'member waybackback when we
wore wristwatches & earth ran on individually

set time?;~ Aunt Notrie drove me to three
Burger Kings just to get that Susie
Carmichael watch that glowed mauve

in the bath suds, so I been knew my
kind could amphibian a way through
white disaster;~ Auntie's tolerance

for smoke, five-hearted as beige earth-
worms, but ma'am;~ what smoke needed
was consequence;~ what it needed

was harm back

for harming;~ whiteness escaped it;~ this
ghetto of angels will not;~ grief is the master
of what happens;~ what girl of color survives

what happens?

Latasha's gravesite in Paradise Memorial Park may have been disturbed in a slew of unearthings initiated by the cemetery proprietors in the '90s. If so, she was exhumed and flung onto a mound with other bone-black remains. The location of the pile is unknown to me, though you know it's a way of reselling plots, of making space for the lucrative business of dying. You know cemeteries know better. You know where this cemetery stay. You got bones to suck the marrow out of when it comes to any paradise. Paradise shouldn't be the name of no cemetery. There are no cemeteries in *Paradise*, the novel. Men shiv women in a convent and when it's time to pile the bodies, our bodies are nowhere to be disturbed. No air. No punishment. Paradise.

5:

When I get to Paradise, the record office is closed. Finding Latasha is entirely up to me.

What I know of this site is its prior owners, their particular horrors—reselling used caskets, occupying single plots with seven or more bodies, stacking skeletal remains behind a tool-shed. In 1995, Aunt Denise met with the cemetery board and was informed that her niece was likely one such body affected. She shared her nightmares with the *Los Angeles Times*:

"All I saw was that big dirt pile
with human bones in it. I didn't go
to sleep until 3 a.m. I came to work today
and I couldn't   concentrate."

There's no inherent logic to the way bodies are lain out here. The dead aren't categorized by last name or date of departure. The lifeless go wherever there's space. A patch of grass the width of my palm is all that stands between one unliving and the next.

Without a guide, I'm left in the wreck of my own strategy. I plan to go row-by-row, starting on the left, working my way to the back in a straight line, then up to the front again. A lawnmoweresque scavenging until I end on the right. I can see the back of Paradise from the entry gate. It's the smallest cemetery on earth to me. I assume speed and ease.

All the headstones are sunken, little molars pounded in their sockets. The cavities collect leaves, Styrofoam cups, the skin of a baseball, a Toyota receipt, soil. When possible, I dust my shoe across the debris. But some stones are so obscured that it'd take hard labor to see them.

Paradise is home to many Black and Brown ancestors. This makes its ragged upkeep a personal slight, an incendiary grief.

I'm patient in the first half hour, considering each stone as if acknowledgment were an apology for my steps, as if I'm weighing on the skulls and femurs of people who still have nerves, thresholds of hurt.

But soon, time augments. August heat, high and unforgiving. I slow and drag an exhausted confidence. Sentimentality leaves, and the earth quits being precious. I skim headstones and keep right on moving. Like Walker shouting Hurston's name in that Eatonville cemetery, I beg Latasha under my breath. *Now come on, sis.* I'm desperate for grace, revelatory light, coordinates conveyed.

After one lap, I'm done with my method. I skip the entire midsection of Paradise and head to the far right, drawn by these tiny handwritten signs on a kudzu brick wall that runs the length of the cemetery. Each sign, a span of numbers.

This makes me think of the memorial ID associated with Latasha's plot on Find a Grave: 181458514. I've always wondered what that number meant. I find a sign on the wall that lists "182–181" and proceed in a line, assuming all graves beginning with 181 will fall in this general vicinity. I'm beside myself with possibility.

I come across the resting place of a baby who lived thirteen days in 1973, two veterans of our last World War, many gone daughters and granddaughters; none of them Latasha.

Now, come on.

Then I think to visit all the plots with offerings. Latasha must be Paradise's most notable soul. There's a mural, a playground, an Oscar-nominated film in her name. How could her grave ever be ordinary, untended?

I stop by all the stuffed animals, peonies, plastic lilies, windmills, water bottles, a wood cutting of "Family," a deflated mylar balloon trilling in the breeze.

I come up hardened, hollow.

The driver who comes to collect me is visibly unsettled, realizing he's arrived at a graveyard. He sees me emerge, pissed off and dark from the tombs, and his first question is if I'm the undertaker.

"I was looking for Latasha Harlins."

"Who?"

When Walker arrived at Hurston's house, she sought the neighbors across the street and, after hearing Hurston's name, that same one-syllable wonder singed the air between them. *Who* is our greatest expectation. A common, cold refrain in the aftermath of our absence.

When I explain Latasha's relevance to the '92 uprising, I can see my driver's smirk from the back of his head. He was fifteen at the time, Latasha's age, and recounts the ransacking of a Sears in Hollywood.

"I remember them stealing TVs. All I kept thinking was why . . . and then I started thinking how I could get me one."

Back at the hotel, I'm thrust into wonder. Is Latasha still in Paradise? Was her body recovered and moved? A Facebook page called Los Angeles Morgue Files suggests she may be resting in Westwood Village Cemetery. No one at the office returns my call.

Then I come across an article in *Whittier Daily News* that mentions the lawsuit against Paradise. After the settlement, city officials erected a tall headstone in the very back of the cemetery to honor those affected by its cruelty. I noticed it when I was in there, but thought nothing of it. The stone stands at a distance from all other graves, on an isle of grass.

According to *Whittier*, this isle is where the majority of exhumed bodies once rested.

I return to Paradise the following morning, three hours before my return flight. I tell the driver, *wait for me, give me three minutes*, and I run to the back of the dead.

Whomever. I take it to mean the city is unaware of who its apology belongs to.

Wherever. As if to say the body may be near, elsewhere, erased, *wherever*—affirming the heartlessness of exhumation, affirming that even if I found Latasha's grave, I would never find her.

And *Forever.*

fraught word, ain't it?

Notes

Arizona?

Page 12

The photo is a still shot from the security camera footage at Empire Liquor Market on March 16, 1991. Sourced from the YouTube video "Shooting of teen Latasha Harlins at Empire Liquor in 1991 (Warning: Graphic content)" by KPCC, 2017.

The text in the upper right is from Judge Joyce Karlin who presided over *People v. Du*. These are remarks she gave during Du's sentencing and a post-trial interview. Sources: *The Contested Murder of Latasha Harlins: Justice, Gender, and the Origins of the LA Riots* by Brenda Stevenson, 2013; *LA 92* by National Geographic, 2017.

The bottom of the collage features excerpts from newspaper coverage of Latasha's murder and the uprising. Much of this text is sourced from Jane L. Twomey's article "Newspaper Coverage of the 1992 Los Angeles Uprising: Race, Place and the Story of the Riot: Radical Ideology in African American and Korean American Newspapers," published in *Race, Gender & Class*, 2001.

In her research, Twomey studied an article titled "A Family Affair" that features an image of a Latinx family taking furniture from a store during the uprising. This brought to mind Sly and the Family Stone's 1971 song "Family Affair." Lyrics from the song are dispersed throughout the poem.

"Tell me what's a black life worth a bottle of juice is no excuse the truth hurts" are lyrics from Tupac Shakur's song "I Wonder If Heaven Got a Ghetto," released on his posthumous album, *R U Still Down? (Remember Me)* in 1997.

Page 15

These photos were taken inside a hair store in North Carolina. At the cash register, the owner displayed photos of shoplifters. The day I entered, two black women named Tanequa and Kierra were pictured.

The text that accompanies the images are lyrics from Ice Cube's song "Black Korea," released on his 1991 album, *Death Certificate*.

Pages 17, 20, and 31

These collages are composed of descriptions and photographs of Black women and girls found on police missing-person flyers and the FBI's Most Wanted list. They reflect the ways Black women and girls are neglected, reduced, and fused together; how we are violently sought after and violently forgotten.

Pages 23 and 24

These passages are ripped from Stevenson's *The Contested Murder of Latasha Harlins*.

A thin obsidian life is heaving on a time limit you've set

Pages 27, 43, 59, 91, and 103

These pieces are based on real Yelp reviews for various minority-owned businesses across the United States.

Pages 28 and 29

The italicized stanzas are from the article "Racial bias in pain assessment and treatment recommendations, and false beliefs about biological differences between blacks and whites" by Kelly M. Hoffman, Sophie Trawalter, Jordan R. Axt, and M. Norman Oliver, published in *Proceedings of the National Academy of Sciences of the United States of America*, 2016.

Page 32

The italicized stanza on the left is a quote from Rozeal, sourced from the interview "Single Works With Myriad Influences," written by Randy Kennedy, published in the *New York Times*, 2013.

Page 37

Much of the text under "CLAIM" and "CONTEXT" comes from the article "What Blacks Fear Most" by David Mikkelson, published on Snopes.com, 2014.

The phenomenon of withholding

Pages 46, 48, 52, and 55

These timelines list names, events, locations, symbols, media, quotes, and stereotypes associated with Black and Asian American communities. These diagrams do not equate experiences but consider them in proximity, observing how racial identities have been shaped and misshaped across time.

Page 50

"You supposed to work for free. Do what black people are supposed to do" is sourced from Stevenson's *The Contested Murder of Latasha Harlins*.

Page 52

The last three italicized phrases are quotes from Donald J. Trump.

"coolest monkey in the jungle" refers to text found on an H&M hoodie worn by a Black child model in 2018.

"wong brothers. a laundry service. 555-wong. two wongs can make it white. abercrombie & fitch" was featured on an Abercrombie T-shirt in 2002.

Page 53

"Someone had to leave the arena to the fools" is based on Toni Cade Bambara's quote "Do not leave the arena to the fools," written in a postcard to Nikky Finney in 1995.

Page 55

This erasure includes quotes from the films *Jackie Brown*, *Do the Right Thing*, and *Menace II Society*. I was interested in the portrayals of Black and Asian American relationships in film, how such portrayals reinforce stereotype and a narrative of opposition.

Page 61

This image of Empire Liquor Market was sourced from the article "Latasha Harlins' death and why Korean Americans were targets in the '92 riots" by Leo Duran, published on KPCC.org, 2017.

Pages 65 and 67

The image of Denise Harlins and her quotes were sourced from the YouTube video "Interview Part 4" by George Chan, 2017.

Citrus visiting me with cruelty

Page 78

My poem "I Am" was published in *A Celebration of Young Poets—Wisconsin Spring 2004*, an anthology by Creative Communication, Inc.

Page 81

The quote from LA Councilmember Marqueece Harris-Dawson is sourced from the article "The killing of Latasha Harlins was 30 years ago. Not enough has changed" by Erika D. Smith, published in the *Los Angeles Times*, 2021.

Paradise

Pages 93 and 94

The italicized stanzas are from Sherman A. James's article "John Henryism and the Health of African Americans," published in *Culture, Medicine and Psychiatry*, 1994.

Page 108

The quote from Denise Harlins is sourced from the article "Families Grieve Again After Graves Disturbed: Families Cope With Renewed Grief, Pain" by Gary Libman, published in the *Los Angeles Times*, 1995.

Acknowledgments

Immense gratitude . . .

To the publications in which many of these poems first appeared: *The Adroit Journal*, *Best New Poets 2020*, *The Chattahoochee Review*, *Guernica*, *Gulf Coast*, *The Kenyon Review*, *The New Republic*, *Pleiades*, and *Poetry*.

To the scholars, writers, artists, and witnesses whose reflections on Latasha Harlins, the LA uprising, and Black and Korean American histories informed *Concentrate*: Brenda Stevenson, author of *The Contested Murder of Latasha Harlins: Justice, Gender, and the Origins of the LA Riots*; Cathy Park Hong, author of *Minor Feelings: An Asian American Reckoning*; Anna Deavere Smith, playwright of *Twilight: Los Angeles 1992*; Dai Sil Kim-Gibson, Elaine Kim, and Christine Choy, directors of *Sa-I-Gu*; T. J. Martin and Daniel Lindsay, directors of *LA 92*.

To those who gave their heart to this project and to me as a writer. These loved ones are vital: Lynnie Holl, Kamilah Aisha Moon, Clarisse Baleja Saidi, Diane Seuss, Malcolm Tariq, Su Hwang, Francis Santana, Teresa Leggard, Aracelis Girmay, Ricky Maldonado, Joy Melody Woods, Jenny Molberg, Chinenyenwa Okoye, Indya Jackson, Yasin Abdul-Muqit, and countless others.

To my educators, Tarfia Faizullah, Tung-Hui Hu, Laura Kasischke, Linda Gregerson, James Davis May, Esther Lee, Karen Gentry, Willie Tolliver Jr., Nicole Stamant, Christine Cozzens, Angelina Cicero, and all who saw my potential and nurtured it early on.

To Rachel Eliza Griffiths whose belief in *Concentrate* is the reason you're holding it. Having her words as the introduction—I couldn't imagine a better birth for this collection.

To everyone at Graywolf, especially my attentive and remarkable editors, Chantz Erolin and Kiki Nicole, who helped this book sing.

To Cave Canem, for opening the door to a legacy of Black poets. I'm ecstatic to be in this family.

To my mother—my love, my support, my all—and to my aunts, my grandmothers, my cousins, the Black women whose knees I sat between, whose lessons I received, whose love and wisdom cover me forever.

Courtney Faye Taylor is a writer and visual artist. She is a winner of the 92Y Discovery Prize and an Academy of American Poets Prize. Her work can be found in *Poetry*, the *Nation*, *Best New Poets 2020*, and elsewhere.

The text of *Concentrate* is set in Sabon Next LT Pro.
Book design by Rachel Holscher.
Composition by Bookmobile Design and Digital
Publisher Services, Minneapolis, Minnesota.
Manufactured by Versa Press on acid-free paper.